What If You Believed?: Turning Trials into Triumphs.

Written by: Donté M. Murphy

I0617386

What If You Believed?: Turning Trials into Triumphs.

In What If You Believed?: Turning Trials into Triumphs, readers will discover a practical framework for transforming life's toughest challenges into opportunities for growth and success. Through personal stories and actionable steps, this book provides inspiration and strategies to turn adversity into triumph.

Written by: Donté M. Murphy

For permissions requests, contact:

Donté M. Murphy

Cover Design: Naeem Khan
Interior Design and Formatting:
Naeem Khan
Published by: DM Publishing

First Edition.

Printed in United States of America.

For more information, visit: trialsintotriumphsbook.com.

Table of Contents

Introduction: What If You Believed?

Discover the power of belief in overcoming adversity.

What if you believed? Truly believed. Not in the way we often say we do, with casual conviction that fades when life takes a sharp turn. But what if you believed in the depths of your soul, with a faith so unshakable that no storm could uproot it?

Life has a way of testing us, of pushing us to our limits. We've all faced moments when the ground beneath us gives way, when everything we've built comes crashing down. The world tells us to give up, to accept defeat, to settle for less. But what if, in those darkest moments, you believed there was more? What if you believed that every setback was just a setup for a comeback?

This book isn't just about my journey—it's about yours. It's about every person who has ever been knocked down and wondered if they could get back up. It's about the power of belief, not just as a vague idea, but as a force that can transform trials into triumphs.

We'll dive into stories of struggle, moments of doubt, and the kind of resilience that comes only when you decide to believe, even when the odds are stacked against you. We'll explore the lessons learned from life's toughest challenges and discover how faith—true, unwavering faith—can turn the impossible into the inevitable.

So, ask yourself: What if you believed? What if you refused to give up, no matter how many times life tried to knock you down? This book will show you that the greatest victories often come from the most challenging battles. All it takes is the courage to believe, and the willingness to turn your trials into triumphs.

Cut From the Court: A Dream Deferred.

Facing rejection and rebuilding after being cut from college basketball.

Exhausted from running 33s, suicides, and Indian sprints for 1.5 hours, Coach finally put us on the court to play 5v5 to see what we had. This was how I started my freshman year of college basketball. But before I get into that, I need to explain where it all started and how I got here. By the age of 10, I had decided in my heart that nothing would stop me from playing professional basketball in the NBA. My favorite player at the time was Jason Kidd, who was averaging 10.8 assists per game that year. My doctor had told me I should grow to about 6'3", which was a great height for an NBA point guard. When I shared my dreams with my mom, she told me it was possible. She reminded me that my cousin, Rob Moore, played in the NFL. I knew his name well—he was a big-time receiver for the Cardinals, and also 6'3". In my mind, it was destiny.

> ***Something to note—*** *I've always remembered that the Bible mentions we should have "childlike" faith. When you think about children, they have so many dreams, so much faith and certainty in their ideas, that they surprise us with what they can accomplish. As adults, life sends us so many trials that we struggle to overcome, or sometimes never overcome, and uncertainty grows with each venture we take, until our default decision becomes to not even try, or we talk ourselves out of it. It's*

> *something we all face and need*
> *to be conscious of— especially*
> *not passing those doubts onto*
> *children.*

To help me reach my goal of becoming an NBA point guard, my dad signed me up for the Philadelphia Sixers camp. It was an amazing opportunity. My dad would drop me off at the gym, and my grandmother "Gramz," who lived in Philly, would pick me up and bring me to her job at Hahnemann Hospital before my dad picked me up again. At the camp, I got the chance to meet Samuel Dalembert. For you Sixers fans, you may remember him as the 2001 draft pick— well, I got to play him 1v1 that summer in a game to 3, and I won. I'll never forget it. He let me score the first time, then I hit a 3-pointer on him, so he started to get serious. On the final point, I gave him a shot fake and went around him for a backboard jumper to win the game. He probably doesn't remember it, but it was a motivating moment in my life. If I never get to meet him again, thank you, Mr. Dalembert.

Playing against an NBA player was incredible, but competing against other campers from the region was even better. It was my first time playing outside of my little South Jersey area. I'd finally see how good I was compared to others. To my surprise, I was the second-best player at the camp in my age group—at least, that was my own estimate. But there was some basis for it. In the 3v3 and 5v5 games, both the campers and coaches kept talking about me and this other kid, a guard from Philly. He was simply better than me at the time. I couldn't stop him from scoring, even with my best "spider" defense, as I called it. He moved so effortlessly and had a fantastic shot fake. After camp, I took some of his moves back with me to South Jersey. I wish I remembered his name—it would be great to see how he turned out.

Now, back to college basketball tryouts. That hour and a half of conditioning was the hardest I'd ever been through. I watched my peers drop out one by one, and as each one left, it made my chances of making the team a little better, pushing me to keep going. I kept an eye on the current players—was there someone I could outlast? I felt like I'd made my presence known. But when it came time to play full-court 5v5, there was nothing left in the tank. And I wasn't alone. All of us who had made it that far were thinking the same thing: *Give the ball up!* We were completely drained but tried to hide it. I can't remember how well I played, but I know the coaches were impressed with our grit. They told us this tryout method had been used for years, and they were surprised that so many of us made it to the end. On the final day of tryouts, only five of us remained—including myself and three friends who had been playing together since the first week of school. We had all set our eyes on making the team, hoping at least one of us would make it.

When the cut list came out, none of us made it—except one friend, and another guy. We called our friend Neo because he was "the one"—a baller from the Bronx. We were all good in our own right, but Neo was the most impactful. He made everyone around him play better, no matter what team he was on. So, when we found out he made the team, it brought some comfort and excitement to our group.

But for me, it hurt. It hurt *bad*. I had never been cut before in my life. Anyone who knew me as a child would tell you my name and basketball were synonymous. I was the kid in third grade playing against middle schoolers. How could this happen? If I couldn't make a college team, how could I ever play in the NBA? Doubt settled in, and I questioned every decision I had made. My first thought was regret for choosing this school over others that had recruited me. I went to Johnson & Wales University in Providence, RI, but I had been recruited to play at the North Carolina campus. I decided to tryout at Providence. What if I had gone there? I also had an offer from a Division II school in Florida, but it didn't offer the major I wanted. Had I made a mistake? What now?

Over time, I have developed a framework to help me turn my trials into triumphs. I will briefly outline the steps here and go into more detail later. My framework is to **SULK, SHOUT, ACCEPT, SMILE, FUEL**, and then **FOCUS**. This six-step process is how I get through tough situations that bring me down and leave me stuck.

SULK:

After learning the news, I went back to my dorm and cried in the shower. It was a huge blow. In my mind, basketball was over for me. How could I ever achieve my lifelong dream if I couldn't even make a college team? After a long shower, I took a drive to clear my head.

SHOUT:

Alone in my car, with the windows up, I shouted—loudly. I was disappointed in myself. I didn't work hard enough. I could have been better prepared. I could have asked current players about the conditioning levels to better prepare myself. If I had been in better shape, I could have shined during the runs and the 5v5, when everyone else was exhausted.

ACCEPT:

It was hard to accept, but what else could I do? I had been cut and needed to decide how to move forward. I called my dad and told him the news. He was disappointed too, but he encouraged me to figure out where I could improve and use that to prepare for next season.

SMILE:

I met with the head coach to get his feedback on my game. To my surprise, he noticed a lot of great things about my play, but he explained why he chose my friend and the other guy over me. One reason was that the other guy had tried out multiple times and showed improvement each year. That gave me the motivation I needed to keep pushing.

FUEL:

Now I knew what the coach thought and understood his reasoning. I knew exactly what I needed to do to make the team next year. My preparation began the next day. My two friends and I hit the courts on a mission. After a week of playing 10+ games a day, we were leaving the gym undefeated. With the conditioning we had just gone through, there was no one who could match us. We shut out teams left and right, winning 7-0, but it still wasn't enough to get ready for next season. I needed more.

FOCUS:

The coach's feedback stuck with me—I wasn't a scorer. At the next level, teams need players who can put the ball in the hoop. My favorite player, Jason Kidd, averaged 10.8 assists per game, and I was more like him— I'd rather pass than score.

Most of my points came from layups or transition baskets. But I needed to score more. So, I started working on my shot every week. During the offseason, I even worked out with some of the basketball players to improve. I found local courts in Rhode Island and competed there too. I made a name for myself and got recruited to play in local men's leagues. When I went back home to New Jersey and dominated the courts, people were surprised when I told them I had been cut from my college team. They were seeing a much better Donté. I was locked in, and nothing could stop me—or so I thought.

Something to note— *in life, some things are out of your control. We don't always know why they happen, but they do. God has a plan, and even if things don't seem to align with what you had in mind, often, if you give it enough time, you'll see how it all led to where you are today.*

Failing Forward: Lessons from College Setbacks.

How academic struggles became the foundation for future success.

For me, college was a time to prove myself and truly set my life path as an adult. No more mommy and daddy watching over me or telling me what to do. As a teenager, I had some autonomy already, so I would say my parents prepared me well for the transition. I was responsible and not easily influenced— qualities that served me throughout college. Still, even the most prepared students face typical pitfalls. Time management, financial stress, and peer pressure can derail even the best intentions, especially during that pivotal freshman year.

Managing time becomes crucial as you juggle academics, social life, and possibly a job. The financial burden of tuition and living expenses can be overwhelming. Overcommitting to activities may lead to burnout, and finding direction for your major can be tough. Peer pressure to fit in or indulge in distractions is always present, and mental health challenges— whether anxiety, loneliness, or stress— must be managed carefully. Recognizing these obstacles is key to surviving college with both your well-being and goals intact.

About 30% of college students don't return after their freshman year, with many struggling academically during that critical first year. Those who require remedial support face even greater challenges, as nearly 75% of them fail to graduate. Although specific figures for students who fail freshman year and later graduate are less frequently reported, early academic struggles often lower the likelihood of finishing a degree (Bird, The Classroom, 2017).

A cumulative of these pitfalls left me failing in my freshman year. I was hit with the reality of being faced with cleaning up my act immediately or being dropped from the university and needing to return home. The thought of returning home was enough threat to get me to take action. See, my older sister didn't finish college, my father didn't finish college, neither did my mother, and in high school I was named most likely to succeed in the yearbook. I had seen many before me go off to college and fall victim to the pitfalls of college. The last thing I wanted to do was follow in those footsteps. I've always been determined to not be labeled or fall into negative stereotypes or statistics.

Coming from where I'm from, the expectations are pretty low.

Even though my desire was to not be dropped from college, I had found myself in this predicament and needed to find a solution and it wasn't going to be something I just will my way. It needed to be intentional if I was going to keep it up and graduate. As I mentioned earlier, I have a specific framework I use to turn trials to triumphs and this scenario was no different.

SULK:

I was so disappointed in myself when my academic advisor told me I was on the brink of being dropped from the university. My heart sank and I couldn't believe that I was doing that badly. Not to mention, I was faced with a potential pregnancy, that ultimately turned out to be a scare. At the time I was unaware. Without feeling comfortable enough to share with my parents and not wanting to fail them or myself. What would my life look like as a 19-year-old college flunky with a child on the way? Will I have to move to another part of the country to be close and raise my child? What would my parents think of me? What would this say about who I am? I was disappointed.

> **Something to note**— I imagine there will be some who would believe the sulking portion isn't helpful, but for me it has been, and here is why. People of faith understand that our struggles aren't just with human problems but with spiritual forces. Negative emotions, though painful, can serve a purpose. By fully confronting

> *and sitting with them, we can quickly release them. Consider the worst possible outcome and ask yourself: how would you handle it? Could you live with the consequences? If the answer is no, it becomes easier to take the next steps toward resolution.*

SHOUT:

Leaving out of the academic office with tears in my eyes, I found myself walking up the street away from the campus to not be seen. I couldn't go to my car, because I had sold it to a friend back home, so where was there to shout? I took the bus to Warwick beach and walked out on the long stone pier. I did not get to shout, but I was able to sit there and cry openly. I was disappointed with myself that I had spiraled and was faced with some really tough decisions and circumstances. However, while sitting there I decided I wasn't going to allow this situation to determine my life outcome.

ACCEPT:

Over the years I've faced some really difficult times, not quite as serious as these, but I was able to get through those, and I was going to get through this one. I was on the brink of failing, but I had not failed yet and if I was to find myself a father soon, I needed to make a change and prepare.

SMILE:

Looking out at the water, a smile appeared on my face, as I thought through what my life could become if I turned my energy and intention to setting my mind on being the best student and father I could become. It created excitement and drew me to shout, "let's get it!"

FUEL:

Feeling like I had hit rock bottom, there was nowhere to go but up from here. I used the weight of my situation as fuel, reminding myself of everything I stood to lose if I didn't turn things around. I tapped into my desire to break the cycle of failure that had impacted my family and prove to myself that I could succeed. Each setback became motivation to push harder, focus on my goals, and take control of my future, no matter how uncertain things seemed. This was my turning point.

FOCUS:

On the bus ride back to campus, I thought about how I was using my time, why I was failing and how I found myself in a pregnancy scare. I set my focus on spending more time studying in the library in odd hours where there's less socializing, reading the chapter before class, asking more questions and seeking how I could apply the learned lessons now to retain the knowledge. I went out and got a job, to have money set aside for the baby, as well as some work experience if I did need to drop out or move.

Later that year I found the pregnancy was just a scare and honestly it was a relief, even though I had come to terms with the idea of being a father I was thankful to not have to take on that burden at 19. A great lesson was learned early, and I'd never find myself in the same predicament again. I also, went on to make dean's list that trimester and every other through graduation. I found that I was a really great student and getting A's actually became easy to me. Another lesson I learned about myself and my capabilities, especially since I barely made the minimal GPA to get accepted into this college.

On the Brink: The Fight Against Homelessness.

Overcoming the fear of losing everything and finding hope in the hardest times.

Heading into my sophomore year of college, I didn't want to stay on campus, and to be honest, my family couldn't get a loan to cover the cost either. I grew up somewhere between poor and probably just under middle class. Originally from Camden, NJ, when my parents were doing okay financially, we moved to smaller towns nearby. But when things took a turn, we would return to Camden. We always lived in an apartment, except for the three times I remember having my own room. That was a luxury for me and my three sisters, so living in a dorm with three other guys wasn't the worst experience, but it was cramped and not worth the money, to say the least.

Before sophomore year started, I managed to get an apartment with two female friends, and we each paid a few hundred dollars a month. This was my first apartment and what some would call the start of the "grown-up" life. In the first semester, things went well. I had a part-time job working at another college nearby in an event staff role for their catering department. The city bus was free, and I used it to get downtown to work or catch the university-provided buses to the other campus for classes.

At some point during the second trimester, I was laid off from my job. It was my first time being laid off, but I later learned this was common, especially as the effects of the 2008 financial crash rippled through the economy. This hit me hard, as I had no other way of making money, and my class schedule made it difficult to get another part-time job. I had about a month's worth of savings left and didn't want to ask my parents for help. I thought I was an adult now, and I wanted to figure this out on my own.

As the final month passed, I was constantly stressed, wondering how I would make money. The weeks slipped by without any substantial way to cover my rent or afford food. Without the catering job, I couldn't eat in their dining halls anymore. I survived mostly on ramen noodles and sold anything of value just to buy myself more time. I was also resourceful enough to eat with friends who would occasionally share a meal swipe with me if we were at one of the dining halls. It was a really stressful time, but I eventually reminded myself of all the things I had accomplished in tough situations when I followed my personal framework.

SULK:

After about a month of sulking over my joblessness and financial struggles, hoping friends would offer free meals, and sometimes going without food, I hit a breaking point. I wasn't even considering going home; my biggest fear was not being able to pay rent and ending up homeless. My room was nearly empty, just clothes and a thin blanket. Without heat, I remember lying in my room, shaking from the cold, wondering if this was going to be my life— cold and alone. I asked my roommates if I could sleep with them for warmth, but they declined my request.

Those thoughts and the harsh reality of my situation weighed heavily on me until I finally managed to pull myself out of that deep sulking state.

SHOUT:

During this tough time, I decided to take the familiar bus ride out to Warwick Beach. It was a chance to escape the cramped apartment and the constant stress. When I got there, I walked out to the pier and just spent time looking out over the water. I didn't shout or make any noise, but standing there, gazing at the horizon, I found the release I needed. The peaceful view helped me gain some perspective and clear my mind. It was a moment of calm that broke through the chaos, giving me the space I needed to move on to the next step of my framework, "ACCEPT."

ACCEPT:

Rent was now late, and I needed to accept the fact I had squandered important time to truly find a solution and might find myself evicted if I didn't act quickly— something that would affect not just me, but also my roommates. Releasing myself from the fear, I was able to think clearly about how I could get back on track and avoid eviction for all of us.

> *Something to note— In life, I've always prided myself on being resourceful, a trait instilled in me by my upbringing. My parents taught me the value of respect, kindness, hard work, and honesty. They emphasized the importance of education and caring for others, which laid a strong foundation for how I*

approach challenges. I draw strength and confidence from my faith, guided by several key biblical principles:

Proverbs 3:5-6 *reminds me to trust in the Lord completely and not rely solely on my own understanding. By submitting all my ways to Him, I believe He will guide me and make my paths straight. This assurance helps me remain confident in my abilities, knowing that I am not alone in navigating life's challenges.*

Psalm 37:5 encourages me to commit my way to the Lord and trust that He will act on my behalf. This verse reinforces my faith that, even when situations seem daunting, if I remain committed and trust in Him, He will support and guide me through.

Mark 9:23 assures me that belief makes all things possible. When I face obstacles, I remind myself that my faith enables me to overcome them. This belief empowers me to persevere, knowing that with faith, nothing is beyond reach.

Matthew 7:11 speaks to God's generosity and willingness to give good things to those who ask Him. This verse encourages me to seek guidance and support with confidence, trusting that God desires to bless and support those who earnestly seek Him.

James 4:3 emphasizes the importance of asking with godly motives. It reminds me to align my requests with God's will and ensure my intentions are pure. This alignment ensures that my efforts and prayers are meaningful and in harmony with divine purpose.

1 John 5:14 underscores the importance of aligning with God's will. I strive to ensure that my actions and requests reflect this alignment, trusting that when they do, I am more likely to receive the support and guidance I seek.

These verses collectively reinforce my confidence and faith in my abilities. They remind me that while I am resourceful and determined, I am also supported by a higher power. The one thing I wish I did differently was to be more honest with my parents and friends about my struggles. I carried on as if everything was fine, but acknowledging my difficulties sooner could have helped me receive the support I needed. Remember, having people to confide in—whether they help you think through challenges or simply offer a listening ear—is invaluable during tough times.

SMILE:

An honest smile appeared on my face as I reflected on some of the resources I had that could help me get back on track. The gloom was over, and I was focused on a positive outcome. I was determined to pay the rent and find new income sources to improve my situation.

FUEL:

Keeping in mind that my poor decisions and slow reaction time could lead to eviction for myself and my two roommates, I sprang into action. There were three ways I knew I could not only make the money I needed but also exceed my previous earnings; working for another school's catering company, participating in an off-campus work-study program, and joining off-campus focus groups/paid studies. Thanks to my connections, I was able to secure opportunities in all three areas within the same week.

FOCUS:

I reached out to friends who were working at a university in Massachusetts during weekends for their catering department. Some of the people from my summer job were working there and often mentioned they needed more help. I was successfully hired at $19/hour, and the work clock began as soon as their van picked us up from the campus courtyard. We'd work about 10 hours a day from Friday through Sunday, which amounted to almost a full-time job. Although it wasn't every weekend, it was at least twice a month. It was the highest hourly wage I had ever received. I also contacted friends who worked in a work-study program at our school and spoke with the program director to find a role at a local middle school during after school hours. Lastly, I participated in focus groups and paid studies at the same university where I had been laid off. By speaking with the right people, I found upcoming studies in the following weeks. Within three weeks, I had paid the back rent and secured upcoming rent, with hundreds of dollars left over. This achievement was a significant win that strengthened my faith for years to come.

Told I'd Never Play Again: Defying the Odds.

How a career-ending injury turned into an opportunity for resilience.

During my junior year, I decided it was time to get back on track and make the basketball team again after dealing with some difficulties and distractions that kept me from trying out my sophomore year. I was finally going to make the team, but I didn't make the cut. Honestly, I wasn't ready, and I knew it. If I was going to make this team, I had to be in a good place and fully committed. So, I started working out every day, focusing on my skills to become a better scorer and an overall better player.

By this point, I had been invited to join some of the team's off-season workouts and was included in their 5v5 runs occasionally. Things were starting to look promising as I continued to put in the work. I hit up the local playgrounds and YMCAs, searching for the best runs I could find in the area. One of the most competitive spots I found was the Cranston YMCA. They had two basketball gyms—one for teens and another on the main campus across the parking lot.

One day, I was playing in the gym, and things got heated. One of the local guys I had battled with on the court many times was talking big, and I was determined to shut him down. After winning several games in a row, he returned to the court, hoping to end my streak. But all game, he couldn't stop me, and I was talking my trash! It wasn't until the final point that he almost had me.

I'll never forget that play. We were up one point and needed two more to win and kick him off the court for good. I drove to the basket, he fouled me, but I pushed through the contact and finished the layup. On the way down, I felt his legs underneath me, and I landed awkwardly on his foot, causing a sharp, intense pain. As I hit the ground, I was certain I had broken my ankle or foot. A crowd of players surrounded me, encouraging me to get up and walk it off, but I knew this wasn't something I could just shake off. However, that same guy was still running his mouth, accusing me of trying to get out of the game before losing. I couldn't let him have that. So, I tied my shoe as tight as I could and got back out there.

On the next offensive possession, I had the ball and hit a jump shot right in his face to end the game. I shouted in excitement as I had come back from injury to prove that, even while injured he still couldn't guard me! It was a great moment, and I earned his respect as a player that day. Little did I know, the fact that I was even moving on that foot was a miracle. As I left the gym and got to the car, the pain got worse with every step, and my ankle started to swell.

I drove to the mall where my girlfriend at the time and our friends were hanging out. After sitting in the food court for a while, everyone eventually left, and it was just me and her. When we went to leave, my foot had gotten to the point where I couldn't stand on it at all.

She knew we needed to get to the emergency room. She actually put me on her back—like a dad does with his kid at a carnival—carried me through the mall and out to the car. I still don't know how she did that, but I guess it was love power, LOL! She didn't have a license, so I had to drive to the emergency room using my left foot while the right one was in excruciating pain. When we got to the hospital, she helped me out of the car and pushed me inside in a wheelchair.

After seeing the X-rays and meeting with the doctor, he told me I had several ligament tears in different areas and would likely never be able to play basketball competitively again.

I was crushed. I had been so close to my goal of playing college basketball. I had been working out with the team, earning their respect, and then—just like that—it was over. This took me a while to process, as you can imagine, but here's what I did:

SULK:

At this point, I had been cut from the team twice, but it finally felt like I was about to make it the next time around. I had put in so much effort, overcoming a lot of personal struggles along the way. Making the team would have made all the trials worth it. But instead, I had the doctor's words ringing in my ears, telling me I'd never play basketball competitively again.

SHOUT:

In this phase, I talked it out with my girlfriend at the time and spent time shouting and crying in my car. I was disappointed in myself more than anything. I remembered the college coach telling me don't play with "non-ballers" to avoid injury, and I didn't listen. That choice felt like it ended my chances of ever having a professional career in basketball—at least, that's what I thought.

ACCEPT:

I spent two months in a boot before I could even walk on it again, let alone play basketball. I had to accept my new reality. Either there was something greater for me than basketball, or this was just another setback for a major comeback. During this time, the idea of "what if?" began creeping back into my mind. What if this wasn't the end, but just a new path outside of college basketball? While I played with the idea, I didn't fully commit to making it a reality, and honestly, I was okay with that.

This injury was the final straw that broke my focus from basketball and shifted my mind to explore business more seriously. I never gave up the game entirely. After getting the boot off, I started my own recovery. It took about three years to regain full flexibility and strength in my ankle, but I continued to play basketball during that time—just not at the highest level.

Since then, I've played in numerous men's leagues, pro-am pickup games, won several championships, and earned respect for my game up and down the East Coast. Even though the injury turned out to be a blessing in disguise, shifting my focus to business, I still find myself wondering, "What if?"

Currently, I coach a varsity boys basketball team in Delaware, at a brand-new high school. This will be our third year, and last year was our first varsity season. We finished 7-13, tying for the best start of a new program. There's still a lot of development ahead, and the team is young, but I'm excited about building a winning culture and leaving a lasting legacy.

Now, as I turn 36 this month, I've decided to give pro basketball one last shot. I'm in almost the best shape of my life and have been able to compete against pros and semi-pro players successfully. Even at this ripe old age, there's still something left in the tank. I want to turn this childhood dream into a reality I can share with my wife, my two sons, and soon-to-be third child. Keep an eye out for the book on that journey.

The Fallout: Growing Up in the Shadow of Divorce.

Navigating family turmoil and finding strength amidst parental separation.

Growing up, my childhood was mostly spent in a two-parent household, but there were times when my parents separated temporarily. These periods of instability and constant moves were linked to their separations, as detailed in the chapter "On the Brink: The Fight Against Homelessness." At the time, I didn't fully understand how these changes were affecting me—it was just my normal. By the time I was 12, my father had moved out for good. Looking back, I can see how deeply these changes impacted various aspects of my life.

My dream of becoming an NBA player was significantly shaken by the upheaval at home. I started to doubt whether I could ever achieve this goal, partly because of a car accident I'll discuss in another chapter and partly due to the reduced time I spent with my father working on basketball. This lack of support and stability began to affect my school performance too. I went from being an honor roll student to a disruptive presence in class during middle school. Even though I still performed well on tests and quizzes, my behavior had drastically changed. I had been a quiet, soft-spoken kid who excelled at basketball, but my new behavior was a sharp contrast to that image.

Research supports that such transitions can have profound effects on children. Studies show that children from divorced families often face emotional and behavioral challenges. Approximately 25-40% of these children experience significant emotional or behavioral problems (National Institute of Mental Health, 2022). Additionally, children of divorced parents are more likely to encounter academic difficulties and behavioral disruptions (American Psychological Association, 2023). The instability and stress from their parents' separation can greatly influence these issues, affecting their overall development and well-being.

As I've grown older, I've reflected on how these early experiences may have shaped my behavior and academic performance. Gaining this understanding has been crucial in my personal journey, highlighting the importance of stability and support in a child's life.

As an adult, heading into my sophomore year of college, I'll never forget the call from my parents. A week after dropping me off at my summer job in Massachusetts, they called to tell me how proud they were of me. But then they hit me with the news—they were getting a divorce. They had already made the decision but waited until my school year ended to tell me. They didn't want the news to affect my studies. At the time, I didn't get why they thought this would shake me up. I mean, by the age of 12, my dad had already moved out of the house permanently, and they had separated plenty of times before. I was 19, living in another state, and planning to get an off-campus apartment before the school year started again.

I remember asking, "Is anything really going to change? Dad, are you still going to be in the same apartment? Mom, are you staying at the same place?" When they both said yes, I couldn't understand how my life would be any different. What I didn't realize was that this divorce meant they were officially moving on. They were no longer hiding behind the idea of marriage or their wedding rings. At the time, it didn't fully sink in, and I didn't notice much of a difference until after college. I had met their "friends" before, but after the divorce, those friends started showing up at important events, sometimes reaching out to me, trying to build a bond. That's when things started to feel a little off for me.

I always wondered, why wait nearly 20 years to get divorced? But after talking with both of them, I understood their reasoning.

They wanted us to grow up with both parents in the house, no matter what. Looking back, our upbringing wasn't perfect, but they raised us well, and we were always loved. There were plenty of things my parents disagreed on, but when it came to raising us, they were aligned.

Now, as a husband with two young kids of my own, I see how easily parents can drift apart when life's problems start piling up. It can feel like everything is turning toxic— can't believe I'm even using that word! LOL. But relationships are hard because they require you to lose some of your individuality and become one. That transition is tough, and it doesn't happen overnight. Knowing how my parents' separation affected me early on made me even more committed to staying together with my wife, to focus on unity instead of retreating into ourselves. It's a prime example of how something negative can inspire positive change. Sometimes, the things you hate going through make you more determined to do things differently.

Something to note— *I must also credit my parents for the faith and relationship with God, they instilled in us. They always reminded us that no matter what happened, God had a plan, even if we couldn't see it at the time. Through their example, I learned that even during the hardest moments, God is working things out for our good. It's tough to trust that when you're in the thick of it, but I've seen firsthand how challenges shape you for the better. My parents taught me that setbacks aren't punishments, they're preparation. They helped me see that every trial has a purpose, and even when life throws you a curveball, there's a bigger plan at play. That understanding has given me the strength to push*

> *through tough times, knowing*
> *that God is in control and, in the*
> *end, everything will work out for*
> *good.*

My parents might see their marriage as a failure, but it was one of my greatest teachers. Through their experiences, I learned the importance of marriage, what it means to be a husband and father, and what to look for in a wife.

This year, my wife and I just celebrated our fourth anniversary and are heading into our fifth. My siblings are all married now, except for one, who is close to making that step too. It's something both my parents are proud of, given that their own marriage didn't make it. I can only imagine the things they went through, the stuff they never told us. Marriage is no joke, but if you stick with it, the rewards aren't just for you; they ripple out to those around you. So, in marriage, I encourage you to always seek unity and be careful not to let self-centeredness lead you astray.

Life at 12: Hit by a Car, Hit by Reality.

The life-changing accident that reshaped my perspective on adversity.

Heading into 6th grade, I was finally a middle schooler, excited for the chance to play for my school's basketball team. I had been playing in recreational leagues, but this was different—the opportunity to compete against the best players from every school. Middle school itself was an adjustment: transitioning from one classroom to multiple, with a real locker. Back in elementary school, I used to watch the middle schoolers play basketball in our yard before heading to their school. I remember being in 3rd grade, playing with them, and now, some of those same guys were in the hallways with me. They knew who I was and were eager to see how I'd do at tryouts.

At this time, my parents were back together again, something that happened often. I had my own room, which was amazing. I had a Nintendo Game Boy, a PlayStation, and a "No Sisters Allowed" rule. We were living in Washington Township, a predominantly white suburb about 25 minutes down Route 42 from Camden, NJ. To be honest, I hated living there, but I had a few friends on my street and the guys I played basketball with, so I made it work. We were the only Black kids in the neighborhood, but we were too young to really understand the racial undertones. In fact, I was the only Black child in my class every year—until middle school. Still, I was excited about middle school basketball and counting down the days until tryouts. Little did I know that opportunity would be cut short.

My parents broke up again, and we had to move right before tryouts. As much as I wanted to play for the school, I was more excited to be moving back to Camden! But that's not where we ended up. We moved in temporarily with one of my mom's friends in Pennsauken, and then to a town called Collingswood, which bordered Camden. I was nervous. I thought it would be another all-white town, like the one where I had always felt so out of place. I finally asked my mom, "Are there going to be any Black or at least Spanish kids there?" I was relieved when she told me she had seen plenty of both when she registered me for school. I was excited! I was finally going to feel comfortable—and still get to play for the school team.

But on the walk to school, I learned something that bummed me out. I wasn't going to middle school after all. This district didn't start middle school until 7th grade. So, I was back in elementary school, but still in 6th grade. When we were let out for recess, I headed straight to the basketball court and found some fellow hoopers. Those same guys became my closest friends all the way through high school.

A few months later, my friend and I were on our way to pick up our sisters from an after-school learning lab, like we did every week. It was a quick walk—maybe six minutes from where we lived. My friend lived on the other side of Route 130, so I called his house a few times to remind him we had to get our sisters, but he didn't pick up. I walked around the corner and crossed Route 130 to find him. He was outside playing. I reminded him, and we started heading to the school. We crossed 130 and were waiting in the median for the light to turn red so we could keep going. When the light finally turned, I took a few steps off the median—and everything went black.

From what I've been told, I was hit by a car that ran the red light going 45 miles per hour or more. My friend, still in the median, stood just 2-3 feet away, watching it all happen. The impact lifted me into the air, and I landed in the middle of the road while the car kept going. I fell on my right side, with a broken pelvic bone, shoulder, and a cracked skull, bleeding out. Witnesses rushed to check on me, while others chased after the car, but I was unconscious and bleeding heavily.

I woke up in the hospital a few days later, in pain, with my family surrounding me. I tried to get up, but the pain was unbearable, and I realized it wasn't a dream. They told me what had happened, and I cried uncontrollably. I had been in a coma, and at one point, it was unclear if I would survive or wake up at all. My family prayed fervently over me, and they were beyond grateful to God when I finally regained consciousness.

I was relieved to be alive, but the pain throughout my body made me doubt I'd ever recover. My dreams of becoming an NBA player seemed shattered. At 12 years old, this was easily the most traumatic experience of my life. It took three days to leave the hospital and return home, but my journey was far from over.

SULK:

Lying in bed, I silently cried myself to sleep many nights after returning home. I thanked God for sparing my life and made a promise: if He would heal me, I would never stray from Him. I started physical therapy to learn how to walk again, using a walker to get around. All I could think about was the day

I'd finally be able to get back on the basketball court.

SHOUT:

There were plenty of times when I'd be lying in my room, silently yelling at God, tears in my eyes, asking, "Why me? Why did this have to happen?" I kept questioning what I could've done to deserve this. Honestly, I never got an answer. But over time, I learned to live with it.

> **Something to note**— I've learned in life, the purpose behind every difficult situation you go through doesn't always come to light quickly or sometimes even at all. You still have to trust that each one was important and a pivotal moment that needed to happen

for something else to occur. In my case, I often wonder what my life would've been like had I never been hit by that car. I don't think I would be as humble or appreciative of life as I am today, understanding how short life truly is and how it can be taken from you in an instant. Then again, maybe this wasn't specifically for me, but for someone else to see their prayers answered through me—or even for the driver of the car that day. I'm not sure, but I'm also okay with not knowing.

ACCEPT:

The accident happened, and I had to face the reality of my recovery. No one was sure when—or if—I'd ever be cleared to play basketball again. There were questions about how long it would take for my head to heal and harden. The uncertainty was difficult, but it was my new reality.

SMILE:

Even though the future of my basketball dream was still unknown, I decided that this accident would become part of my testimony—a way to share God's grace and favor in my life. That testimony would be more powerful and reach more people than I ever could through basketball.

FUEL:

After months of physical therapy, I finally ditched the walker. It was a huge moment for me. I was determined to run and play basketball again, so I pushed myself harder every day to get stronger.

FOCUS:

I had gained weight during my recovery, so I started walking to shed the extra pounds. Walking turned into jogging, which eventually became sprinting. By the time summer came around, I was back on the basketball court with my friends, working on my game. By 7th grade, I was cleared by my doctor to play, and I made the middle school basketball team as a starter. It was an incredibly satisfying moment. Even though I wasn't as good as I had been before the accident, I was one step closer to my dream.

Work or Play: Choosing Between Passion and Survival.

Balancing high school sports with the necessity of earning a living.

With my father out of the house, I had become "man of the house," a term I'd hear many times. I didn't really understand what that meant at the time, especially since I wasn't responsible for paying rent. But as I grew into my teenage years, I realized being the man of the house meant one thing—you need to provide. When my father left, I took on the responsibility of looking out for my sisters and my mother. Early on, I'd walk my younger sisters to school, make sure they stayed on top of their homework, and check who their friends were to keep them on the right path. This was my role as an older brother, but over time, it evolved into financial provision.

It started small. I'd do odd jobs like shoveling snow or cutting grass to make a few bucks to contribute to the household, sometimes bringing my sister along so she could get a cut too. But as I got older, the need felt bigger to me. What began as $10 or $20 here and there turned into a few hundred dollars when I started working. It felt good to take care of my family in whatever way I could, but I didn't realize the implications of spending more time working and less time playing basketball.

As the years went by, I went from starting point guard in middle school to sitting on the JV bench in high school. I was still a good player, but some of my peers started to pass me. They had an impact in games that kept them on the court longer than me. By the time I made varsity, my coach pulled me aside. He said he commended my desire to work for my family, given my situation, and the staff had been very understanding and lenient with me. But ultimately, he said I needed to make a choice—work or high school sports.

I was torn. Should I follow my dream, or keep supporting my family? The fact that I even had to make this decision frustrated me. I blamed my father for leaving and not fighting to come back, like he had done before. I blamed my mother, too, for putting this pressure on me, even though she did it in the softest way possible. I had to choose, and something had to give.

In the end, I decided to continue working and gave up my shot at playing varsity basketball.

It was a tough decision, but I figured the coaches didn't really care about me anyway. They weren't that interested. I had seen them go out of their way for other guys on the team in worse situations than mine. Plus, I wasn't going to get much playing time, so what was the point? I might as well give up on basketball and move on.

Every time I started to make progress, something got in the way. This time, it was my family—they needed me when I needed help myself. So many nights, I broke down in that apartment while sleeping on the couch so my sisters could have their own room. I lived out of a portion of the closet, with no bed. I remember asking myself, *why is this my life? Why can't things just be normal?* I was so fed up with it all, I decided I was going to run away. I was too afraid to actually do it, so I told my mom I was leaving, but instead, I hid in the closet for hours. I stayed there so long that I fell asleep.

When I woke up in the middle of the night and climbed out, everyone was peacefully asleep. No one missed me. My mom just figured I stayed at a friend's house. I felt useless, like I had no purpose. That was the first time I seriously thought about committing suicide.

I didn't know how I'd do it, but I wanted it to be painless. I remember holding a knife to my wrist, but I couldn't bring myself to do it. Staring at myself in the mirror, crying, I wondered what would happen if I died. How would my sisters go on without me? What would my mom do? I did so many little things that were important, but I never felt appreciated. It was just expected of me.

Something to note— *Today, suicide prevention and mental health awareness are constantly talked about. But I often wonder, how could someone have stopped me from committing suicide that day, if I had decided to go through with it? I've never figured that out. No one would have known— I was pretending to be happy while I was suffering inside. I even joked about my situation like it wasn't a big deal, when it really was. If anything, I've learned to look out for those who seem the strongest. There's probably something going on, and you might be the only person who notices and reaches out. That small act could save a life, even if you never realize it.*

That year, I convinced my parents to let me have the car my father had parked in the back of our apartment lot. It had been damaged in a flood years earlier, but I committed to getting it fixed so I could go anywhere I wanted.

Growing up, my mom always told me, "If you have a driver's license, you can get anywhere. But if you have a car, you can go when you want." That stuck with me. The pressure I felt at home made me really want to get away. Having a car also meant I could get a job further away and make more money.

Heading into my senior year, I left my job at Taco Bell, started my own eBay shop, and worked part-time at K-Mart. For several months, I was making $3,000 a month while still playing AAU and attending school. That period really shifted my focus toward business more than basketball. It was the first time I seriously considered a career path that didn't involve the game.

Laid Off Again: Bouncing Back from Career Shifts.

Dealing with professional setbacks and finding new direction after EAW.

After graduating from college, I began interviewing with several companies, looking for the next role to catapult my career and prove myself in the corporate world. During my senior year, I was offered a full-time position at a printing and marketing franchise to help build their mobile website and email marketing business. They were already generating millions in revenue, and I was brought in to add to those millions. I enjoyed the role, the autonomy they gave me, and the opportunity to turn many of my ideas into proof of concept. However, I was ready for a larger challenge in a more corporate setting.

One of the companies I interviewed with was Eastern Acoustic Works (EAW), for a Marketing Coordinator position. It was an entry-level role in their small marketing department, and they needed someone sharp, ready to work, and with a strong background. I was the perfect fit. After several rounds of interviews, I was offered the job—my first corporate role, and I was determined not to disappoint.

Without delving into too many details, the marketing director and I transformed the way we approached marketing at the company. We moved away from the traditional trade shows and advertising, focusing instead on a more B2C approach, as opposed to the typical B2B strategy everyone else in the industry was using. We redesigned the website, making it more user-friendly and aesthetically pleasing, started blogging, and created spoof social media accounts that gave us a unique voice in the industry. We allocated some of the funds we saved toward "road shows"— live events where prospects and clients could experience our sound systems firsthand, rather than just discussing the technology at a trade show booth. This approach was unheard of, but it worked. When we launched our new, industry changing product, the same magazines that once charged us to advertise were now offering free coverage. Our blog and social media presence exploded, and everyone in the industry was eager to see what we were working on.

We introduced the new product at Coachella, the perfect venue to bring top influencers for a live demonstration. For those who don't know, Coachella is a major music and arts festival held annually in Indio,

California. It features a diverse lineup of top artists and is known for its vibrant atmosphere, art installations, and influential fashion. Beyond music, it offers unique brand experiences, food, and parties, making it a key cultural event.

The event was a success. We closed deals that weekend, and the momentum carried us for months. My director and I were riding high on the success we had created within just a year. As we approached my one-year anniversary, I was sure a raise or bonus was in the cards.

I'll never forget that morning. I walked in excited for the day, turned on my computer, and got to work. My director hadn't arrived yet, but when he did, he tapped me on the shoulder and asked me to meet him in the conference room. I thought, "This is it! The

CEO is going to congratulate us and offer a raise!" I walked in smiling, but my director was there with HR, and the look on his face was concerning.

He explained that he had asked HR to let him deliver the news. He went on to tell me what an amazing job I had done, but that we were being laid off. It wasn't due to our performance, but the company had made the decision regardless of our success. I was given a severance package, approval for unemployment filing, and a small box to gather my things. Just like that, I was no longer employed.

SULK:

In my young career, it was really unsettling. I couldn't understand how a company could let go of a marketing department that had not only saved them money but also increased revenue and significantly boosted brand awareness in just one year. The more I questioned it, the more frustrated I became.

SHOUT:

I thought, "These people are idiots!" We had done all this work, only for them to toss us aside and ride the wave of everything we created. How was this fair? I had invested so much energy into this company, only to be discarded at the drop of a hat. I hated the feeling.

ACCEPT:

The words rang over and over in my head—
"it's not based on performance..."If it wasn't,
why would they do this? I couldn't
understand it, but I had to accept it. I had
worked two jobs in two years, and now I was
back in the job market, having to explain
these short stints, no matter how great the
accomplishments.

SMILE:

After many interviews, it became tiresome to
explain the layoff, but I always found it funny
that I was being paid unemployment. This
company was contributing to unemployment
when they could have just kept me
employed. I was making them far more than
they were paying me.

FUEL:

Those months of unemployment gave me time to improve my interview skills, quickly establish rapport in conversations, and effectively highlight my successes. I also learned how to best explain my accomplishments when applying for higher-level roles.

FOCUS:

I decided to use this period of unemployment to sharpen my communication skills, earn some certifications, and refine my resume for more senior roles. It took me five months to land my next job, but I jumped from an entry-level role to senior management with a significant pay increase. That layoff, as painful as it was, set me up for a big leap forward!

Facing the Truth: When Color Becomes a Barrier.

Confronting racial challenges and overcoming societal limitations.

I went through the phone interviews, and they were great. I scheduled an in-person interview with the hiring manager, feeling excited about my chances. It seemed like I was going to get the role! Little did I know, this interview would open my eyes to what racism really is. Early in my career, after being laid off from EAW, I was searching for another opportunity and came across a marketing role at a nationally recognized jewelry company. It seemed like the perfect fit.

When I met the hiring manager, everything went smoothly. We discussed the role, the company's growth, and how my skill set aligned with what they needed. It was the first time in my career where the employer had researched me and tried to convince me the role was a great fit. It felt amazing— a dynamic I had never experienced before. Later in my career, I would learn this is how companies treat potential employees who they believe will be pivotal to their success.

But despite how well everything went, it didn't end with an offer. Instead, it ended with the statement, "You have a color problem."

At the end of the interview, the hiring manager leveled with me. He said, "I'm not going to lie to you. You're the best candidate I've seen in years. You're professional, extremely knowledgeable in marketing and business, and you have an amazing track record. But I have to be honest. The owner is a good friend of mine, and he won't let me hire you. It's because you have a color problem."

That's a phrase I'll never forget. It didn't upset me, but it opened my eyes to a few things: 1 – How deep racism runs, 2 – How present it still is, and 3 – It is never going away. While someone else might have been appalled, I remember smiling and saying, "I know. I've had it and will always have it as long as I live here."

Something to note— Biases and disadvantages will always exist. If you're honest, you have your own biases too. They're frustrating and disheartening when they affect you, but a mantra I've always lived by is, "You can't control what happens,

> *but you can control how you respond."*

I've faced racism many times in my life, and you'll read more about that in another book. But my response has always been the same: "Now it is time to level up." Honestly, facing racism directly has helped me refine the framework I've used to turn trials into triumphs. Here's the internal dialogue and how I applied the framework in this situation:

SULK:

Wow. Could he have been any more direct? My name and voice over the phone got me to the in-person interview, but my face wasn't white enough to get the job— even though he admitted I was the most qualified. How long will I have to live with this reality? Is it even worth trying anymore?

SHOUT:

Why does this country still hate us? What have we ever done to deserve this? America claims it was built on judging character, not skin color, but we're nowhere near that ideal. The promise of equality hasn't been fulfilled. There's still too much judgment based on race and not enough focus on who we are inside. America was supposed to be different, but we've got a long way to go to live out that dream.

ACCEPT:

Racism and biases will always exist. I'd rather know where someone stands upfront so I can decide how to move forward sooner. This won't be the last time it happens, so I need to figure out how I'll handle it. Getting upset doesn't change reality.

SMILE:

The hiring manager showed me how great I really am, and that lifted my spirits. There have been plenty of interviews where I didn't get the job, and I never knew why. It may not have always been racism, but I'll never forget another interview I had with an Asian woman. She couldn't believe the person in front of her was the same "Donté Murphy" she had spoken to on the phone. LOL.

FUEL:

There's nothing I can do about racism except push past the barriers it puts in front of me. The more they try to stop me, the stronger I become. That's been my fuel for success for years, and it's a source that never runs out.

FOCUS:

Each time I experience racism, it sharpens my focus. It makes me even more intentional about improving my skills, making more money, or becoming more successful. I hope that by doing so, I'll eventually find myself in rooms where my face is accepted, and I can have the impact I've always set out to make.

> ***Something to note—*** *Racism is undefeated in a lot of ways. Its main strategy is to put obstacles in front of you, hoping you'll give up and believe you don't belong. There have been moments when I've felt that pressure, but I always remind myself of the people who died fighting for the freedoms we take for granted. I hope to be an example for anyone who feels like they can't*

win against racism, for those who wonder, "Why even try?" If I can find success in my life, I hope others will see that and be inspired to keep pushing through too.

Breaking Free: Heartbreak and the Post-College Journey.

Overcoming emotional loss and regaining focus after a major breakup.

I had my moments of uncertainty, but there was never any real evidence to make me think something was wrong in the relationship. However, the messages I saw on her phone screen, while sitting in my car, were everything I needed to understand that this relationship was over.

During my junior year of college, I was doing well. I had improved in basketball, playing with the team in the off-season, running my business, and working. Academically, I was on the dean's list; I had money, and it looked like I was back on the path to pursuing my dream of basketball. It was a short fall break,

and I decided to head home. While visiting, I
received a message from a girl I went to high
school with. It had been years, and we
decided to meet up. I learned she was
planning to attend the same college as me in
the winter, but at a different campus. When I
got back to campus, we talked often, and
eventually, she decided to attend the same
campus as me. At the time, there seemed to
be some interest, but I wasn't too sure. I was
also quite the popular guy at college and on
a great path to success – I wasn't looking to
settle down.

Regardless of those thoughts, within a few
months of her arrival, we found ourselves in
a relationship. We went on to have a 4-year
relationship with many great memories, but
it ultimately ended in a breakup. She came to
know all of my darkest secrets, inner
thoughts, and successes in life. I was certain

she would be the woman I'd make my wife. During that 4th year, I was dealing with the EAW layoff I mentioned previously and the decision to leave the job I took afterward. I decided I was done working for companies in the area and started looking for jobs back in New Jersey. It was Thursday, and I had an in-person interview with a company in North Jersey on Friday.

Before heading out, I dropped my girlfriend off at her job and started making my way to 95 South. A few minutes into my drive, I heard her phone go off in the passenger seat. She had left it behind. I opened the phone and saw a text message from a guy's name I didn't recognize. When I opened it, I found out she had been seeing him for a few months behind my back. In disbelief, I turned around and dropped the phone off at her job, leaving it with a co-worker, with the screen open so my now ex-girlfriend could see what I saw when she got the phone.

SULK:

Finding those messages on her phone was like a punch to the gut. Everything seemed to be falling into place, and I thought my relationship was solid. But this betrayal threw me off balance. I felt lost and confused, unable to make sense of how something so important could crumble so suddenly.

SHOUT:

"How could she do this to me?" I screamed inside. The person who knew me best had shattered my trust, and I was left grappling with the unfairness of it all. That weekend, I was making a deposit on the engagement ring I had designed. Why would God allow the relationship to go on for this long, only for it to end like this? It was infuriating and felt so unjust. I thought I was doing everything right, but the person I trusted most was sneaking around behind my back.

ACCEPT:

It took me a few years to get over the breakup before considering another relationship, but I accepted we wouldn't get back together the day we broke up. Some things come to an end, and it's important to accept that realization quickly. No one wants their relationship to end, but sometimes they do, and sometimes they need to. In our case, we both went on to do great things separately, and no ill will exists between us.

SMILE:

Reflecting on the years gone by, I found myself grateful for the many experiences that shaped me, especially those influenced by her. That chapter of my life had closed, but it was crucial in preparing me for the current chapters I'm writing. This journey serves as a constant reminder that "all things work together for good," as each experience has contributed to who I am today and the path I'm on.

FUEL:

My motivation to keep going wasn't based on anger toward her or the situation but rather on reflecting on the impact she had on my life. Regardless of how it ended, I knew I was better in a relationship, and it was meant for me to be married. There's great value in having a wife, and I knew there were many things I needed to change to be suited for marriage.

FOCUS:

I needed to become a better leader and example in order to prepare for a relationship and ultimately a wife. Once I stopped the distractions, focused on my purpose, and let God lead the way, I met a great young lady who would eventually become my wife.

> ***Something to note—*** *I'm not providing this level of detail to take a stab at anyone, but rather to share the experience, the impact it had on me, and how I handled it. To this day, there's no bad blood between us. To be honest, there never has been*

since that day. We are all imperfect people, and the quicker you understand that the easier it is to accept your own faults before looking at someone else's. As heartbreaking as it was for me to deal with, from the many trials I experienced leading up to that point, I knew this too would set me up for a triumph.

Loss and Legacy: Dealing with the Death of Loved Ones.

Coping with the tragic loss of Phoenix, Matt, and Derrick, and finding healing.

Death is an inevitable part of life, but it's often one of the most difficult things to endure. For me, I've attended more funerals than the number of years I've lived—by the time this book is published, I'll be 36. That's a lot of grief, tears, and loss for one lifetime. Yet, it's my reality. And despite going through it so many times, none of them have become easier. If you're wondering if repeated loss gets easier, toss that idea out. It's just as painful every single time.

There are three deaths that have impacted me the most—Phoenix, Matt, and Derrick. Each was one of my best friends at the time

of their passing. All around my age and
thriving in their life. I often found
myself asking, "Why them? Why now? Why
would God take them so soon?"

Phoenix was the first. We met during our
freshman year of college. She was from
Randallstown, MD, a suburb outside
Baltimore, and lived in the same dorm as me.
She was also a culinary student. I'll always
remember her as tall, beautiful, a track star,
kind, and wise beyond her years. She had a
southern tone and was the voice of reason in
my ear, always reminding me I could do
better when I was navigating the freedom
college life brings. We stayed close after
graduation, talking often. The last time we
spoke, she was venturing into
entrepreneurship, starting a baking company
with a mutual friend. She was also engaged
to a guy we knew from college. Things were

going great for her, and I finally had the chance to tell her how proud I was. We ended the conversation with plans to meet up and celebrate our success. I had no idea that would be our last conversation. She passed away in a car accident shortly after.

I was devastated. Phoenix was young, kind, and had so much life ahead of her. There were so many more things we needed to do together, memories to make, milestones to celebrate. Those opportunities were taken from me, but I had to trust God had a purpose. At her funeral, I saw how many lives she had touched. So many of us from college were there, excited to see each other, but heartbroken that this was the reason for our reunion. We promised to stay in touch, but as time passed, communication became less frequent. Phoenix's family created Random Acts of Kindness cards in her memory, honoring the small gestures she was always known for. Though she's no longer here, those gestures continue. Even after her death, I found myself in quiet moments, having imaginary conversations with her. She was always there, consoling me, telling me it would be okay. I'll always miss her.

Matt was a skinny, funny kid I met in middle school. He was the life of the group and a master storyteller. No one could hype up even the simplest story like Matt could. He'd have you on the edge of your seat, eagerly waiting for what came next. We stayed close through high school and beyond. We spent weekends at each other's houses, took trips with his mom to conferences, and had a blast. When I moved back to New Jersey, Matt and Derrick were always at my apartment. We were the three amigos, inseparable.

One day, I got the call: "Have you seen Matt?" I had a bad feeling in the pit of my stomach. Later that day, a few of our friends, including Derrick, broke into Matt's house through the garage. They found him in his room; he had passed away the night before. It was a huge blow to all of us. Our group of friends, known as "The Camp," were devastated. We never imagined any of us dying so young. Matt didn't make it to his 30th birthday. He had recently started a new management role and was on track to become a regional manager. He left behind young children who would never see their father again. It was a heartbreaking loss for everyone who knew him. Another friend I'll never share new memories or life milestones with. Again, I found myself asking God, "Why them? Why now?" But I never got an answer.

The last, and probably the hardest loss I've experienced, was Derrick. He was my best friend since the age of 12. He was the first person I met when my mom moved us to Collingswood, and we later found out that our mothers had been best friends growing up. When Derrick came over to work on a school project one day, my mom recognized him and asked if his mother's name was Barbera. Our mothers laughed and reminisced about old times, just like Derrick and I would do as we got older.

Before Derrick passed, I was so proud of him. He had gotten into coaching basketball and football at our old middle and high school, even pulling me in to help coach basketball. We won championships together, and while I moved on to coach at a college, Derrick stayed and thrived. He also started a sports training company, helping student-athletes and adults get in shape. His business was growing rapidly, and he was on track to hit six figures doing what he loved. I couldn't have been prouder.

When I got the call asking, "Have you seen Derrick?" my heart sank. I hoped it wouldn't be true, but it was. He passed away just like Matt. He was taken to the hospital, but he didn't make it.

Each of these losses hit differently, and losing loved ones can be crippling. It can cause you to slow down and stall your progress in life. I've seen friends struggle to move on, sometimes fighting guilt, thinking they could have done something to prevent the death. Those thoughts can be so dark they pull you down to a place you can't escape. My hope is that the framework I'm sharing will help you through the pain of losing a loved one, so you can live a life they would be proud of.

The Leap: Leaving Corporate to Pursue My Purpose.

Breaking free from the corporate world to follow a higher calling.

I had quite the career in corporate America. Over the years, I learned so much about myself, met many great people, and accomplished significant things across multiple industries. My career path was never traditional, and I later realized my abilities weren't either. I transitioned from industry to industry, role to role, consistently achieving success. I helped my employers improve their bottom line from my position within the company, time and time again. Each new role presented a greater challenge, but they all led to a point where there was no more vertical growth without waiting years.

I discovered I had a natural ability to understand a business, identify process issues, and solve them. From bottleneck sales constraints to poor email marketing practices that led to low open rates, or website designs that deterred users from buying, I resolved them all, quickly. It was exciting, and I felt great knowing I was helping corporations solve complex problems. I was useful and important in their eyes, something I had always desired.

The success and pay were great, but I had to contend with major issues in corporate America—most notably, jealousy and a racist undertone. As mentioned before, my goal was to find rooms where my face was accepted, allowing me to be as impactful as I had set out to be. While I successfully reached those rooms, the people I reported to often worried that I wanted their job or would outshine them. This was never my intention, but I learned through mentors that such insecurity was common in the corporate world. I made it clear I wasn't aiming to replace them, and I constantly highlighted their successes, even giving credit when it was my work. Still, I encountered the same challenges at each company until I had enough.

At one company, the director I reported to had been hired by the owner. He took credit for everything I did well but blamed me when things went wrong. In our check-ins, he often belittled me and questioned if I deserved my salary. He made racist comments, which I initially overlooked. Eventually, he tried to justify a pay cut by moving my position to a smaller office outside the city, even though the original salary increase was based on working in the city. This was the final straw. I went to HR, but they were hesitant to act because the HR manager was on contract and feared losing her job due to the director's friendship with the owner.

Frustrated, I wrote to the CEO, hoping for a resolution, but nothing changed. I met with HR and my director one last time and agreed to resign with severance. That was the last straw for me—I vowed never to return to corporate America.

SULK:

I was angry. I couldn't believe I had to deal with this, and I didn't understand why. I had pushed through so many barriers, but this one was different. Was I not as strong as I thought? Was this something I'd always face in corporate America?

SHOUT:

My frustration reached its peak, and I decided I would never work in corporate America again. This was the tipping point I needed to make a change in my career, which led to some of the greatest successes of my life.

ACCEPT:

I recalled a phrase I had heard: "Go where you're celebrated, not where you're tolerated." I had to accept that the goals I wanted to reach weren't attainable within a company.

SMILE:

Despite the bitterness of leaving, I felt good knowing I had exited on my terms. I left with my dignity intact and addressed the issues head-on. My work—content I created, SOPs, and marketing strategies— would live on. Even though I was gone, my impact remained, and I could point to those accomplishments for years to come. Interestingly, almost eight years later, the company still uses some of the processes I created.

FUEL:

Reflecting on my accomplishments made me realize how much I enjoyed the work and the impact I had. I decided I could still work with corporations, but as a consultant, not an employee. I had unique skills that could benefit organizations while being lucrative for me.

FOCUS:

I set out to find clients who might be interested in my services, and I found success quickly. My first client was a massive Fortune 100 global company. I created the website, sales structure, marketing strategy, and SOPs for a new business unit they were establishing. That unit is now instrumental in their global product adoption, and I'm proud to have played a role in their growth.

Something to note— *God's divine power has already given you everything you need—whether it's within you or accessible through Him. By believing this and stepping into that truth, you realize that no obstacle is too great and no challenge too overwhelming. When you tap into the resources He's provided, both inside and around you, you unlock the ability to live with confidence and purpose, knowing you're equipped for whatever life throws your way. I've always believed this, and acquiring my first client as a consultant is one of my favorite examples of putting this into action.*

The First Fall: Lessons from My Failed Business Venture.

How the Local Merchant Book taught me the value of failure and resilience.

After leaving corporate America, I moved back to New Jersey to start a new venture as a corporate consultant, where I found great success helping companies achieve their goals. Confident from my consulting work, I decided to try my hand at entrepreneurship, thinking that if I could help corporations thrive, surely, I could do the same for myself. Boy, was I wrong. The skills that made me an excellent analyst and consultant didn't automatically translate into running my own business. When you're in the thick of it, it's hard to see the challenges from the inside.

The first business I ever started was Local Merchant Book, a physical coupon book full of offers from local businesses, which would be used as a scholarship fundraiser for high schools. My model was simple: 100 Camden County, New Jersey businesses would include their coupon(s), and the 26 high schools would sell them for $20, earning thousands of dollars every quarter and providing each school with a larger amount of scholarship funding for seniors across the county.

I had built an email list of thousands of patrons interested in the book, but I struggled to get schools and businesses to buy in. Growing up, I remembered the Entertainment Book—it was $20, had like 1,000 coupons, and was a great fundraiser. But that was years ago, and the times had changed. Small businesses were left with very few patrons from the Entertainment Book, and overall sales had dropped significantly for the schools. I struggled to get them to understand the difference between my books.

My big business idea was failing miserably, and I ultimately had to close the business and return the funds to the businesses that had already paid to participate. This hurt me a lot. It was the first time I had failed in a business sense. All the success I had in corporate didn't help me in this venture, except for building a large email list. Without someone else's budget, I had to figure out how to succeed on a shoestring budget, which was incredibly difficult. While the list was created, I didn't know how to get the businesses and schools to participate. I felt like a failure for giving up on the business.

Sometimes you have to know when to get out or pivot, but it's finding the key takeaways you can apply next time that makes it not a failure. This was something I didn't understand at the time, but I would come to recognize it later.

From that business failure, I went on to open a marketing agency aimed at addressing common pitfalls small businesses face, such as lead generation and customer acquisition. That business is still active and inspired me to start a website design firm. This firm works with non-profits to strengthen their online presence, boost donations, and also increases web traffic for small businesses. With two offices and a growth rate of over 200% year-over-year, the firm has seen significant success. While these businesses aren't discussed in the book, I wanted to provide an update since the failure of Local Merchant Book.

SULK:

After leaving corporate America and returning to New Jersey, I was full of hope, ready to dive into entrepreneurship with my first venture, Local Merchant Book. But when the business started to fail, I sank into a period of sulking. I had left behind a stable career for what I thought would be an easy success. Instead, I found myself unable to convince enough schools or businesses to participate, and my excitement turned to disappointment. The gap between my corporate success and my new entrepreneurial struggle was overwhelming. I felt like I had failed not just in the venture, but in understanding the challenge itself.

SHOUT:

Once the weight of failure set in, I reached a breaking point. I remember one night after another round of rejections from businesses, I just let it all out. I didn't shout out loud, but I vented my frustrations through late-night texts and long phone calls with friends, explaining how lost I felt. It wasn't just about the failed business—it was about realizing that the skills that made me successful in corporate America didn't translate as seamlessly as I thought they would. That release was necessary. It helped me process the shock and start to clear my mind.

ACCEPT:

After that emotional release, I began to come to terms with the fact that my first business venture was not going to succeed. I had to accept that, despite my corporate background, entrepreneurship was a different beast. I recognized that this failure didn't mean I wasn't capable of succeeding in the future. It was simply a lesson I had to learn the hard way. Acceptance was difficult because it meant swallowing my pride, returning the funds, and closing the business I'd invested so much hope in.

SMILE:

The turning point came when I started reflecting on what I had achieved, even though the business itself failed. I had built a large email list of potential customers— something that could be valuable in future ventures. I smiled as I realized this wasn't a total loss. I hadn't failed as a businessperson; I had just learned what doesn't work. And in that realization, I found a small victory, a glimpse of hope that my next idea might succeed because of these hard-learned lessons.

FUEL:

With a renewed sense of purpose, I began to focus on the lessons I had learned from Local Merchant Book. I took the time to improve my entrepreneurial skills— learning about sales strategies, customer engagement, and how to better tailor my pitch to both businesses and schools. I refined my approach to building partnerships, and those failures became the fuel that motivated me to try again, this time with a deeper understanding of what it really takes to succeed in the business world.

FOCUS:

Armed with new insights and lessons from my failed venture, I shifted my focus to the future. I realized that entrepreneurship requires resilience, strategy, and a deeper understanding of the market. I wasn't giving up; I was simply recalibrating. With the knowledge I gained, I could now approach new ventures with clearer goals and a more realistic plan. I was more focused than ever on what I needed to do next—no longer discouraged by the past, but motivated to turn this trial into a stepping stone for future success.

> ***Something to note—*** *This chapter highlights an important truth: failure is part of the journey. My corporate background didn't automatically make me a successful entrepreneur, and that's okay. What mattered was how I responded to failure—by learning from it, accepting the lessons, and applying them to future efforts. There's value in every setback, as long as you're willing*

to extract the wisdom from it and use it to fuel your next move.

Turning Trials Into Triumphs: The Framework to Thrive.

Introducing the SULK, SHOUT, ACCEPT, SMILE, FUEL, and FOCUS framework.

As we reach the final chapter, it's important to reflect on the journey you've been on. Life's trials often seem like impossible obstacles, but they don't have to define us. Instead, they can become the foundation for our greatest triumphs. This framework is designed to help you navigate the emotional rollercoaster that comes with adversity and find your way to a place of strength, resilience, and purpose. Each step is a reminder that hardships are not the end, but a beginning—a process that can transform you into a stronger, more focused version of yourself.

In this chapter, we'll break down the six steps of this process: SULK, SHOUT, ACCEPT, SMILE, FUEL, and FOCUS. Each phase has its purpose, from feeling the weight of your trials to releasing your frustrations, accepting your reality, finding moments of hope, gathering the strength to move forward, and ultimately locking in on a path to victory. These steps have guided me through my toughest challenges, from childhood injuries to near homelessness, and they can do the same for you. This framework is about turning your lowest moments into fuel for growth, pushing forward with clarity, and embracing the triumphs that lie ahead.

SULK:

This is where it all begins. In this step, you allow yourself to sit in the discomfort, to feel the weight of the trial in front of you. It's not about giving up; it is about taking the time to recognize that something is wrong and letting yourself experience the emotions that come with it. It's okay to sulk for a bit, to feel frustrated, sad, or disappointed.

- *Example*: When I was hit by a car at age 12, I had to sulk in the reality that my life had changed. I couldn't play basketball, couldn't hang out like I used to. That initial period of sulking was necessary for me to process what had happened.

SHOUT:

Once you've felt the full weight of the situation, it is time to shout. This does not always mean literally yelling, but it does mean releasing the emotions you have been carrying. This could be through a long run, a hard workout, or a moment of vulnerability where you let it all out. Shouting is about taking control of the emotions that felt uncontrollable in the sulk phase.

- **_Example_**: During my sophomore year of college, when I was nearly homeless and broke, I took a bus to Warwick Beach just to shout. I sat at the edge of the pier, let the tears flow, and allowed myself to release the stress and frustration. It was the release I needed to keep going.

ACCEPT:

After the shout comes acceptance. This is the turning point. Acceptance doesn't mean you are okay with what happened, but it does mean you're ready to face it. You stop resisting reality and start to see what is next. In this phase, you say, "Okay, this is what it is, but it is not the end."

- ***Example***: When my parents divorced, it took time for me to accept that my family was forever changed. But once I did, I realized I could either let that pain define me or I could decide what kind of person I wanted to become despite it.

SMILE:

Once you embrace acceptance, you start finding reasons to smile again. It's about recognizing small signs of hope, even while you are still going through the hardship. A smile shows that you're learning something from the experience, maybe even being shaped in ways you didn't anticipate. It's a shift in how you see things—a moment to pause and take a breath.

- **Example**: After being nearly homeless, I finally landed a job. It wasn't my dream job, but that first paycheck brought a smile to my face because I knew I was taking steps toward getting back on my feet.

FUEL:

Smiling gives you the energy to move forward, and that's where fuel comes in. In this step, you gather the motivation, resources, and strength to overcome the trial. Whether it's leaning on your faith, finding inspiration from past wins, or seeking support from loved ones, fuel is what powers your next move.

  - **Example**: After being laid off from EAW, my fuel came during those months of unemployment. I used the time to significantly improve my interview skills, learning how to quickly spark rapport and keep conversations flowing. I also honed my ability to clearly explain the successes I had in meeting the requirements for higher-level roles.

This newfound confidence and skill set became the driving force behind my motivation to find new opportunities and advance my career.

FOCUS:

With fuel in your tank, it's time to focus. This step is all about locking in on the actions you need to take to turn the trial into triumph. You have gone through the emotions, accepted the situation, and found the strength to move forward. Now, you channel all of that into a clear, determined path toward success.

- ***Example:*** After nearly losing everything in college, I focused on getting a steady job, sticking to my classes, and rebuilding. That focus turned what felt like the lowest point into a moment of triumph because I kept pushing forward with clarity and purpose.

This framework is all about moving through the hard stuff—letting yourself feel it, release it, accept it, and then turn it into something that fuels you forward. Each step gets you closer to transforming trials into triumphs.

Closing Note.

Thank you for joining me on this journey through What If You Believed?: Turning Trials into Triumphs. I hope that the stories and insights shared within these pages have inspired you to embrace your own challenges as opportunities for growth and transformation. Remember, every trial you face is a stepping stone toward a greater triumph.

As you continue on your path, I encourage you to explore additional resources designed to support and enhance your journey. Our companion journal and workbook, based on the SULK, SHOUT, ACCEPT, SMILE, FUEL, and FOCUS framework, are crafted to help you apply the principles discussed in this book to your own life. These tools offer practical exercises and reflections to guide you in turning your trials into triumphs.

To access these resources and more, please visit trialsintotriumphsbook.com. You can also scan the QR code below for direct access.

Thank you for believing in yourself and for taking the steps to turn your trials into triumphs. The journey may be challenging, but the rewards are worth it. Keep pushing forward, and never forget that your greatest victories often arise from your deepest struggles.

With gratitude and encouragement,

Donté M. Murphy

About the Author

Donté M. Murphy is an accomplished author, business owner, and marketing expert dedicated to helping individuals turn their trials into triumphs. With over 12 years of progressive experience in marketing and management, Donté has built a successful career around his expertise in digital marketing, lead generation, and business development.

As the Chief Marketing Director at **Conglomerate Marketing Agency**, Donté oversees digital content creation, client acquisition strategies, and marketing campaigns that drive brand awareness and revenue. His leadership has led to a 30% increase in sales and a significant expansion of the company's operations. Additionally, Donté is the founder of **6Ninety9 Web**

Design, a firm specializing in web design and development that helps businesses establish their online presence with impactful and functional websites.

Donté's professional journey has also included roles with notable organizations such as Worldwide Clinical Trials, Arkema, Microsoft, and Animal Welfare Association, where he honed his skills in email marketing, compliance projects, and fundraising campaigns. His diverse experience has equipped him with a deep understanding of various industries and the ability to craft effective marketing strategies.

In addition to his professional achievements, Donté is a dedicated high school Varsity Boys Basketball Coach. His commitment to developing young athletes and fostering team spirit reflects his belief in the power of perseverance and teamwork, which he also applies in his book.

In *What If You Believed?: Turning Trials into Triumphs*, Donté shares his personal framework for overcoming adversity, drawing from his own experiences of navigating challenges such as being cut from his college basketball team, facing near-homelessness, and dealing with personal and professional setbacks. His book provides readers with practical tools and insights for transforming their struggles into sources of strength and growth.

Donté is also a devoted family man, living with his wife Alicia and their two sons, Levi and Preston. His family has been a source of unwavering support throughout his journey. He is grateful to his parents and sisters for their encouragement and belief in his vision.

For more information about Donté and to access additional resources, including a journal and workbook based on the framework in his book, visit trialsintotriumphsbook.com.

Acknowledgements.

Writing this book has been a deep personal journey, and I am grateful to many individuals who have supported and inspired me along the way.

First and foremost, I want to express my heartfelt gratitude to my wife, Alicia. Your unwavering love, support, and belief in me have been the foundation of my strength and resilience. You have been my rock through every challenge, and this book would not have been possible without you.

To my sons, Levi and Preston, your joy and curiosity are my constant sources of motivation. You inspire me every day to be better and to strive for greatness.

I am deeply thankful to my mother and father for their unwavering support and guidance. Your encouragement and belief in me have shaped who I am today. To my sisters, thank you for your constant support and for always being there to lift me up.

A warm thank you to my friends and mentors who have provided invaluable guidance and wisdom. Your insights and feedback have been instrumental in shaping this book.

I am especially grateful to the readers who have shared their own stories and challenges with me. Your experiences have enriched my understanding and reaffirmed my belief in the power of turning trials into triumphs.

To the professionals who contributed to the book's design and formatting, your expertise has brought this project to life. Thank you for your dedication and hard work.

Finally, a special thanks to everyone who has supported me on this journey, whether through encouragement, inspiration, or simply by being there. This book is as much yours as it is mine.

With deepest gratitude,

Donté M. Murphy